D0948980

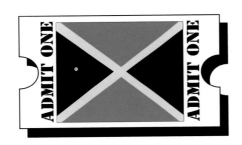

EMMA S. CLARK MEMORIAL LIBRARY
SETAUKET, L.I., NEW YORK 11733

Caribbean Sea
From Port
Antonio

FACES
AND
PLACES

JAMAICA

BY MARY BERENDES

THE CHILD'S WORLD®, INC.

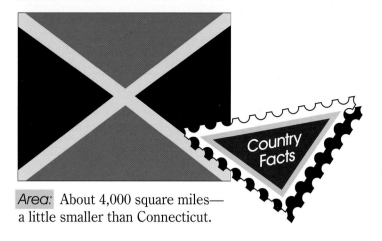

Country Facts

Area: About 4,000 square miles—a little smaller than Connecticut.

Population: About 2,600,000 people.

Capital City: Kingston.

Other Important Cities: Montego Bay, Negril, Ocho Rios, Port Antonio.

Money: The Jamaican dollar. One Jamaican dollar is divided into 100 cents.

National Language: English.

National Song: "Jamaica."

National Holiday: Independence Day on August 6.

National Flag: Four triangles of green and black separated by yellow stripes. The green stands for hope and good farming. The black stands for hard times. The yellow stands for the bright sun that shines on Jamaica.

Chief of State: Queen Elizabeth II of Great Britain.

Head Of Government: Prime Minister Percival James Patterson.

Text copyright © 1999 by The Child's World®, Inc.
All rights reserved. No part of this book may be reproduced or utilized in any form or by any means without written permission from the publisher.
Printed in the United States of America.

Library of Congress Cataloging-in-Publication Data
Berendes, Mary.
Jamaica / by Mary Berendes.
Series: "Faces and Places".
p. cm.
Includes index.
Summary: Describes the geography, history, people, and customs of Jamaica
ISBN 1-56766-515-2 (library bound : alk. paper)

1. Jamaica — Description and travel — Juvenile literature.
2. Jamaica — Social life and customs — Juvenile literature.
[1. Jamaica.] I. Title.

F1877.2.B47 1998
917 — dc21
97-49952
CIP
AC

GRAPHIC DESIGN
Robert A. Honey, Seattle

PHOTO RESEARCH
James R. Rothaus / James R. Rothaus & Associates

ELECTRONIC PRE–PRESS PRODUCTION
Robert E. Bonaker / Graphic Design & Consulting Co.

PHOTOGRAPHY
Cover photo: Portrait of Young Jamaican Girl by Tim Thompson/Corbis

Table
of
Contents

Where Is Jamaica?

From outer space, Earth looks like a big, blue ball. At a closer look, you can see many things. The blue is really oceans and lakes. The white streaks are really clouds. There are lots of brown and green patches, too. These are land areas. Earth's land areas come in many sizes. The biggest land areas

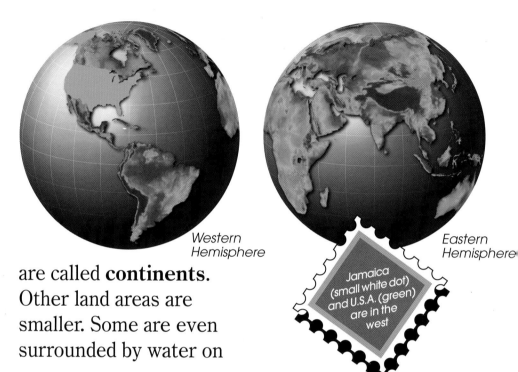

Western Hemisphere

Eastern Hemisphere

Jamaica (small white dot) and U.S.A. (green) are in the west

are called **continents**. Other land areas are smaller. Some are even surrounded by water on

all sides. These land areas surrounded by water are called **islands**. Jamaica is an island. It is also a country.

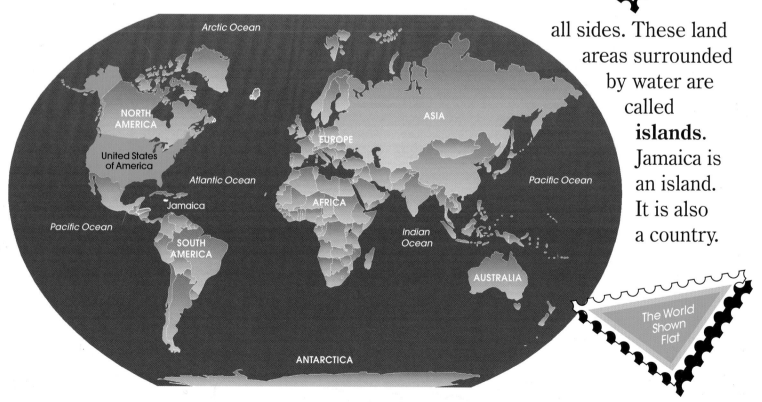

Arctic Ocean

NORTH AMERICA

United States of America

Atlantic Ocean

Jamaica

Pacific Ocean

SOUTH AMERICA

EUROPE

ASIA

AFRICA

Indian Ocean

Pacific Ocean

AUSTRALIA

ANTARCTICA

The World Shown Flat

Close-Up
of
Jamaica

CUBA

HAITI

JAMAICA

Caribbean
Sea

Negril

Dunns Falls

Black River

Port Antonio

Palm Trees
On Beach
At Negril

Eye Ubiquitous/Corbis

Tropical Island
Off Port
Antonio

Reinhard Eisele/Corbis

Jamaica is a very beautiful place. There are green mountains and beaches of white sand. There are also lots of sparkling rivers and waterfalls. Jamaica is a **tropical** island, which means that the weather is warm all year long. It rains a lot there, too. The warm, wet air is perfect for growing plants and trees. In parts of Jamaica, jungles grow green and thick.

Black
River

Dunns
Falls

Bojan Brecelj/Corbis

Bob Krist/Corbis

Plants of all kinds can be found in Jamaica. Trees such as mahogany, cedar, and coconut palms grow in many areas. Banana and mango trees are common, too. Tropical flowers such as orchids live in Jamaica's forests. And green plants such as ferns grow almost everywhere.

Kit Kittle/Corbis

Many types of animals make the island their home. Birds such as cuckoos, parrots, and hummingbirds live in the green jungle trees. Frogs, crocodiles, and lizards are found in Jamaica, too. And in the clear ocean waters along the shore, turtles, rays, and colorful fish swim and play.

Caribbean Parrot At Ocho Rios

Never insult a CROCODILE Until after you've crossed the River

Buddy Mays/Corbis

Sign At Crocodile Farm Near Falmouth

Sting Ray Near Old Pirate City Of Port Royal

Stephen Frink/Corbis

Falmouth

Ocho Rios

Blue Hole

Port Royal

Diver
Among Fish
At Blue
Hole

Jeffrey L. Rotman/Corbis

Edinburgh Castle ∴

★Kingston

Colonial Devon
House In
Kingston

Eye Ubiquitous/Corbis

Ruins Of Edinburgh Castle

Bojan Brecelj/Corbis

The first people to live in Jamaica were called the *Arawak* (AIR-uh-wak) people. They lived happily for hundreds of years. But over time, explorers and settlers from other countries came to Jamaica. They took away the Arawak people's land and made them work as slaves.

Soon many of the Arawak slaves became sick and died. People from the country of Africa were brought over to replace them. The African slaves were treated very poorly. They were forced to work hard in the hot sun and sticky weather.

Ruins Of A Sugar Mill

African Native Shopping Area In Kingston

Hulton-Deutsch Collection/Corbis

Bojan Brecelj/Corbis

Because of the hard-working slaves, Jamaica soon became a very important island. The country of Great Britain took over the government and began to rule Jamaica. But Great Britain soon realized that slavery was wrong. After many long years, the slaves were finally set free.

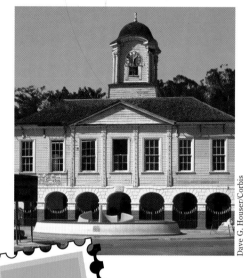

Dave G. Houser/Corbis

Lucea Courthouse

Today, Jamaica has its own government. It works with the people to make safe laws for the country. But Jamaica's government still works closely with Great Britain's government, too. The two countries work together to make Jamaica a safe and peaceful place.

Outskirts Of Kingston

Reinhard Eisele/Corbis

Dave G. Houser/Corbis

Ian Fleming's House, Golden Eye

14

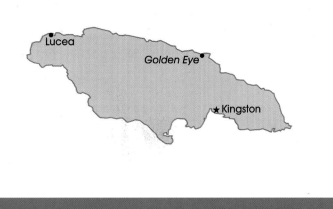

Lucea

Golden Eye

★ Kingston

Capital
Of Jamaica
Is
Kingston

Eye Ubiquitous/Corbis

Bradley Smith/ Corbis

Style Of
Dress
May Be
Inherited

Montego
Bay

St. Anns Bay

★Kingston

Most Jamaicans are relatives of the African slaves. Others are relatives of the settlers and explorers. And some people are relatives of both groups. As Jamaica's cities begin to grow, more and more **immigrants**, or newcomers, are coming to Jamaica, too. Many come from places such as China and India.

Mike Zens/Corbis

Happy Group From St. Anns Bay

Dave G. Houser/Corbis

Rastafarian From Montego Bay

Ethiopian Orthodox Church Members In Kingston

Daniel Lainé/Corbis

City Life And Country Life

Montego Bay Shanty Town

Howard Davies/Corbis

Jamaica's cities are much like those in the United States. There are hotels, offices, and restaurants. There are markets and shops. There are busy streets, too. Some city people have lots of money. They live in nice houses with big yards. Other people are poor. They often live in crowded, noisy areas.

Jamaica Palace Hotel Courtyard

Reinhard Eisele/Corbis

Life in Jamaica's countryside is different. Instead of big houses, people live in small, simple homes. Many of the roads are too narrow for cars, so people walk or ride bikes to get around. And in the mountains, many homes do not have electricity. Even so, Jamaica's country people live there comfortably.

Family Home Near Spanish Town

Jeffry W. Myers/Corbis

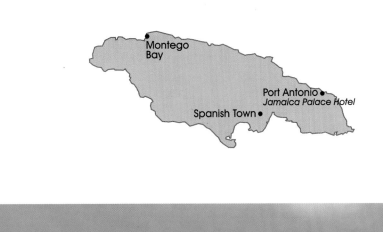

Montego
Bay

Port Antonio
Jamaica Palace Hotel

Spanish Town

Reinhard Eisele/Corbis

Trident Hotel In
Port Antonio

Montego
Bay
● Savanna la Mar

Port Antonio ●

★ Kingston

Mike Zens/Corbis

Students
Cool Off
In Montego
Bay Pool

Jamaican children begin school when they are about six years old. They learn math, science, and English just as you do. Classes begin between 7:30 and 9:00 in the morning. By 2:00 in the afternoon, classes must end. That is because Jamaica's afternoon sunshine makes it too hot for the students to learn very well.

Dave G. Houser/Corbis

Jamaica's main language is English. English was brought to the island by the settlers from Great Britain. But Jamaican English is a little different from what you are used to. That is because most people speak a form of English called a **dialect**. In the Jamaican dialect, English and African words are mixed together.

Students At School In Savanna la Mar

School Class Near Port Antonio

Kingston Student Sculps Woman's Head

Mike Zens/Corbis

Hulton-Deutsch Collection/Corbis

Work

The people of Jamaica have many jobs. Some work on farms raising sugarcane or bananas. Others grow coconuts and yams. Some people work in markets selling fruits and vegetables. Others pick coffee in huge green fields.

Tony Arruza Corbis

Cleaning Crayfish In St. Elizabeth Parish

Some Jamaicans work in factories that produce clothes, shoes, and molasses. And many others have jobs in hotels, restaurants, and shops. Jamaicans are hard workers!

Lady Truck Driver Near Kingston

Howard Davies/Corbis

Aluminum Refinery Worker In Mandeville

James L. Amos/Corbis

St. Elizabeth Parish
Mandeville
Kingston
Blue Mountains

Coffee Farmer In Blue Mountains

Howard Davies/Corbis

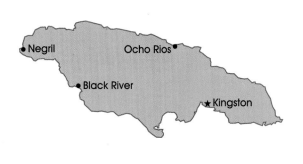

Negril •   Ocho Rios •

• Black River

★ Kingston

Patio Lunch In
Ocho Rios

Stephanie Colasanti/Corbis

Shopping Market In Kingston

Daniel Lainé/Corbis

Jamaicans love to eat fresh fruits and vegetables such as bananas, yams, mangoes, and pumpkins. They also like foods such as beans and rice. The most famous dish in Jamaica is called *jerked pork*. To make it, bits of pork are covered in a thick, spicy sauce. Then the pork is cooked over a barbecue. Many Jamaicans also like jerked chicken.

Cutting Jerked Chicken In Negril

Dave G. Houser/Corbis

Reinhard Eisele/Corbis

Black River Produce Stand

Young Diver Off Port Maria

Like most other countries around the world, Jamaicans love to play soccer. They also like to play a game called *cricket*. Cricket is a British game that is a little like baseball.

Another game, called *dominoes*, is very popular, too. To play Jamaican-style, players slam their dominoes down on a hard table. SLAP! With any luck, the slamming scares the other players. It makes it hard for them to think. Then the player can try to win the game.

Dave Bartruff/Corbis

The Bob Marley Museum Honors The Reggae Musician

MARLEY ROAD

Eye Ubiquitous/Corbis

Cricket Team Tryouts In Falmouth

Jonathan Blair/Corbis

Eye Ubiquitous/Corbis

Falmouth

Ocho Rios • • Port Maria

Bob Marley
Museum

Relax At
The Beach
In
Ocho Rios

Lucea
Grand Lido Resort

★ Kingston

Jimmy Carter Presidential Library/Corbis

Boys Watch
Parade In
Kingston

Holidays

Jamaicans celebrate many of the same holidays we do, such as Christmas, Easter, and New Year's. They also have many celebrations of their own. One special day in Jamaica is Independence Day. On this day, there are lots of parades and music. People sing and dance merrily. Independence Day in Jamaica is a little like our Fourth of July.

Jamaica is a land of cool, green mountains and hot, sandy beaches. Perhaps you will visit this sunny island someday. If you do, try a few things Jamaican-style. Play in a cricket game or eat some jerked pork. Dance to a cool Jamaican tune, or swim in the clear blue water. Whatever you decide to do, Jamaica is sure to keep you happy!

Young Festival Goer From Lucea

Eye Ubiquitous/Corbis

Dave G. Houser/Corbis

Sunny Beach At The Grand Lido Resort

Did You Know?

One popular style of music in Jamaica is called **reggae** (REH-gay). Reggae music has a slow beat and lots of guitar sounds. The words of reggae songs often talk about how people should be fair to one another.

Some Jamaicans wear their hair in long knots or braids called **dreadlocks**. They are meant to make people think of a lion's mane. Just like the lions of Africa, dreadlocks stand for power, pride, and freedom.

The national bird of Jamaica is a kind of hummingbird called the Doctor Bird. It lives only in Jamaica. Its beautiful feathers are very shiny. When the sunshine hits its feathers, the Doctor Bird shimmers with every color of the rainbow.

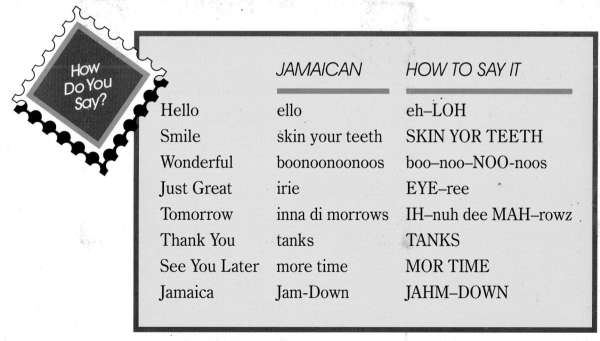

How Do You Say?

	JAMAICAN	HOW TO SAY IT
Hello	ello	eh–LOH
Smile	skin your teeth	SKIN YOR TEETH
Wonderful	boonoonoonoos	boo–noo–NOO-noos
Just Great	irie	EYE–ree
Tomorrow	inna di morrows	IH–nuh dee MAH–rowz
Thank You	tanks	TANKS
See You Later	more time	MOR TIME
Jamaica	Jam-Down	JAHM–DOWN

Glossary

continents (KON-tih-nents)
The biggest land areas on Earth are called continents. Some continents are made up of many different countries.

dialect (DY-uh-lekt)
A dialect is a different form of a language. Jamaicans speak a dialect of English.

dreadlocks (DRED-loks)
Dreadlocks are long, twisted braids or knots of hair. Dreadlocks remind people of a lion's mane and stand for power, pride, and freedom.

islands (EYE-landz)
Islands are areas of land that are surrounded on all sides by water. Jamaica is an island.

immigrants (IH-mih-grents)
Immigrants are newcomers from other countries. Many Jamaicans are immigrants.

reggae (REH-gay)
Reggae is a style of music. The words of reggae songs often talk about unity and fairness to others.

tropical (TRAH-pi-kull)
A tropical area has warm weather all year long. Jamaica is a tropical island.

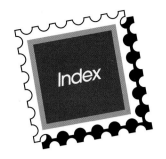

Index